First Published in Great Britain by

Lyrical Scotland, an Imprint of Cauldron Press Ltd
Parton House Stables
Castle Douglas
Kirkcudbrightshire
Scotland
DG7 3NB

www.lyricalscotland.com

Photographs copyright Allan Wright 2008
Introduction copyright Allan Wright 2008

isbn 9781905683369

British Library Cataloguing-in-Publication Data
A catalogue record for this book is available on request from the British Library

Layout and captions and repro by Allan Wright
Page make up by Small Print, Castle Douglas
Printed in Poland

for Lorna

SCOTLAND'S WEST COAST

AN ODYSSEY

PHOTOGRAPHS BY ALLAN WRIGHT

Introduction

The term 'west coast' is one of those preciously generic terms in the Scottish consciousness. Used to describe an area as loosely defined as anywhere between Kintyre and Sutherland, the term has a colourful and seductive resonance to it, and is an expression I have heard often for as far back as I can remember. I can still hear voices from the past saying, "I think I'll take a trip up the west coast" as if it were a sure remedy for the pressures and burdens of everyday life. There is a ring to it, an instinctive suggestion that over to the west lies the promise of a wondrously sensual and invigorating experience, an experience there is really no excuse to miss out on at some point in our lives.

I have spent a significant portion of my life buying into that notion, and have been pounding the windswept trail on the land and shores between the Mull of Kintyre and Sandwood Bay in Sutherland over a period of about 18 years. This book is a collation of the best moments I have experienced on the west coast in that time - edited highlights, if you like. I think of it as a personal odyssey, my purpose in travelling here being to uncover an essence of place. I am happily aware that this is a never-ending quest, a task I shall never complete, as this landscape delivers *ad infinitum* all manner of spectacular moments and breathtakingly subtle beauty. All I have to do is be there and keep my eyes and heart open.

In the main I travel with my faithful companion Tara. Her Labrador instincts have been honed over the years, and together we roam and seek out our different quarries. Hers are, of course, olfactory, while mine are visual, but she understands the game and the rules. Our travels are mainly undertaken by means of a simply converted van or elderly camper van, a supremely independent mode of transport that offers unparalleled simplicity and flexibility, enabling us to pitch camp and start the day right where the action is. When the light is good and ongoing I can get so involved that Tara has to remind me when it is time for us to eat. At other times, when the Scotch mist descends, there is no better place to contemplate quietly and catch up on some reading. It is rare for the weather on the west coast to be stuck for long, as the restless Atlantic delivers a constant change of conditions, often at very short notice.

The images in this book are sequenced from South to North, with brief excursions onto the islands of Arran, Islay, Jura, Mull, Iona, Tiree, Coll and Skye. The regions covered are Argyll, Lochaber, Wester Ross and Sutherland. However, I make no attempt to be thorough in my presentation of the many virtues each of these places possesses. The book is not intended to be a catalogue of beauty spots, but rather a series of inspired moments linked by my insatiable desire to define the humbling beauty of Scotland's west coast. I hope that the images convey the pure exhilaration of those chance encounters in which fleeting light and serendipitously arranged objects in the landscape conspired to create truly magical moments.

Scotland at its best or West Coast forever - enjoy it whenever you can.

Allan Wright

May 2008

Pirates Cove, Corrie, Isle of Arran

West Coast

May morning in Glen Sannox with mists clinging to the Goatfell mountain ranges,
Isle of Arran.

Sannox Beach sweeps round the bay under the presiding mass of Goatfell, Arran.

West Coast

Tropical colours of the crystal waters lapping upon the Corrie shore, Arran.

Above: Basking seal and Ailsa Craig, Kildonan Shore, Arran.

Opposite: Sunrise at Pladda and Ailsa Craig from Kildonan, Arran.

West Coast

Three principle Neolithic standing stones at Machrie Moor, Arran.

Sunset and a drifter, Kilbrannan Sound, Blackwaterfoot, Arran.

Catacol Bay, Arran.

Skipness Castle, Kintyre, Argyll.

Carradale Bay, Kintyre.

West Coast

Saddell Bay, Kintyre.

Left:
The Linda McCartney
Memorial Garden,
Campbeltown.

Opposite page:
Working vessels at
Campbeltown Harbour
and Davaar Island.

Carskey Bay, Mull of Kintyre.

Bellochantuy Bay and Paps of Jura, West Coast of Kintyre.

Sunset on West Loch Tarbert.

East Loch Tarbert, Tarbert.

Feral Goats, West Coast of Jura.

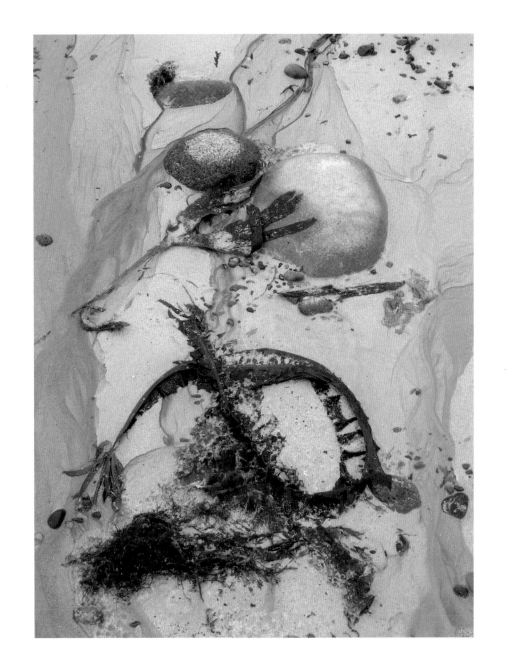

Beach detail, Saligo Bay, Islay.

Portnahaven, Islay.

East Loch Tarbert.

Moorings and Flag Iris, Kames, by the Kyles of Bute and Tighnabruaich.

Tighnabruaich and The Kyles of Bute.

Wild flowers on the shore with Arran on the horizon, Kilbride Bay, Cowal Peninsula, Argyll.

Gulf stream waters sustain a luxuriant kelp bed at Ascog Bay, Cowal.

Houses on the promenade, Dunoon, Cowal.

West Coast

Dunoon Pier with Jupiter the Gourock Ferry and the Waverley paddling back "up the watter" to Glasgow.

*Ardkinglas Woodland
Garden, Loch Fyne.*

Acer, Bluebells and Eucalyptus bark, Crarae Garden NTS, Loch Fyne.

Inveraray, Loch Fyne, Argyll.

Rhododendrons, Crarae Garden, NTS, Loch Fyne.

Crinan Basin, Crinan Canal.

Bellanoch Moorings, Loch Crinan, Crinan Canal.

Above: Vernacular cottage and sky, Kilmory, Knapdale.

Opposite: Shafts of golden light over Jura from Keilmore, Knapdale.

Last light, moorings at Tayvalich, Knapdale.

Carsaig Jetty, Tayvalich, Knapdale.

Cattle grazing by Loch Sween looking to Jura, Kilmory, Knapdale.

The 12th Century Castle Sween.

Dunadd ancient fort and capital of ancient kingdom of Dalriada, by Kilmartin, Mid Argyll.

Lone ketch slips quietly up Loch Craignish to Ardfern as the sun sets over Luing, Shuna and Mull.

Bridge over the Atlantic, Clachan, Isle of Seil.

Looking back to Easdale from Easdale Island, Montbretia glows in the late warm sun.

The Columba Hotel and beach, Oban, at dusk.

Hogh Bay looking to Rum and Skye, Isle of Coll.

West Coast   51

Highland Ponies catch the first rays, Caolas, Isle of Tiree.

Driftwood stranded at Hynish, Tiree.

Gothic mists swirl around Kilchurn Castle, Loch Awe.

Shady Highlanders, near Portsonachan, Loch Awe.

Above: The renowned Oban Swans in the bay at dusk

Opposite: Fresh snow, Ben Cruachan from by Fearnoch, Loch Etive..

A confident windswept Highlander poses at Duart Castle, Isle of Mull.

A wee clinker built dinghy in its own wee sandy bay, St Ronan's, Isle of Iona.

The quintessential West Coast sunset,
Calgary Bay, Mull.

Cave, pebbles and kelp at the "Wilderness Beach", Ardmeanach, Mull.

Above: Road to Loch Buie and Ben Buie, Mull.

Opposite: Seaweed in rock pool, Ardmeanach, Mull.

Castle Stalker, Appin, Loch Linnhe.

Tumbledown sheep shack, Isle of Lismore.

Loch Linnhe and the Morvern Hills, Port Appin.

Sunset over Mull and Lismore from Port Appin.

May and rhododendrons run amok in the lower reaches of Glen Etive.

Buachaille Etive Mor, Glencoe. One of the best known and iconic Scottish mountains.

The Pap of Glencoe peeks splendidly above the tranquil water of Glencoe Lochan.

Stormy light burns its way up the dark glen, River Coe and rainbow, Glencoe.

Classic West Coast mooring, Bishops Bay, Isles of Glencoe, Loch Leven.

Warm light breaks through the cloud, Loch Leven from Kinlochleven.

Above: Lone Birch stands defiant against the backdrop of Ben Nevis, from Sgurr a Mhaim, Mamores.

Opposite: Ben Nevis rises majestically above Loch Linnhe, viewed here from the south at Inverscaddle Bay..

West Coast

Right: Glenfinnan Viaduct and Loch Shiel.

Opposite: The Jacobite Steam train crossing the Glenfinnan Viaduct. Completed in 1901 the viaduct was one of the first major concrete structures and built by Sir Robert McAlpine.

The Jacobite steam train passing Polnish Church by Lochailort on the "Road to the Isles".
This is considered to be one the finest railway journeys in the world.

Steam train snakes its way along the banks of Loch Eilt.

Heather and a copse of Scots Pines preserved upon a tiny islet on Loch Eilt.

The romantic setting of Castle Tioram,
Loch Moidart.

Atlantic sundown,
Sanna Bay, Ardnamurchan.

Silhouette of the Sgurr of Eigg, sunset at Arisaig shore.

Estuarine tranquillity near the Silver Sands, Back of Keppoch, Arisaig.

Rich colours, cries of seagulls and the reek of fish define the ambience of Mallaig Harbour.

Bog cotton grasses bob and flutter in the breeze of high summer, Sandaig Bay, Knoydart.

Dawn light diffuses through the Caledonian Canal at Glen Loy.

The snow clad Five Sisters of Kintail at the head of Loch Duich.

The Glenelg Tractor.

Highland cottage and garden, Glenelg.

A vintage blue boat moored by Eilean Donan Castle, Loch Duich.

Above: Castle Moy, Kyleakin, Skye.

Opposite: Eilean Donan Castle at Dusk.

Cattle on Shore, Loch Scavaig and the Cuillins, Elgol, Skye.

Village of Plockton and Loch Carron.

Above: Scotch mist descends upon Plockton Bay.

Opposite: Ceol Mor momentarily catches the last light of the day in the this exquisite cove, Plockton.

Loch Carron from above Plockton looking to the Crowlin Islands, Rasaay and the Cuillins of Skye.

Sheep and cottage, the shore by Lochcarron.

A broad sweep of rivulets ripple and sparkle across the red sand beach at Applecross.

The tiny hamlet of Ard Dhubh nestles on its own small promontory, Applecross.

An exhilarating drive round the coast north from Applecross affords access to some very special places such as this vernacular cottage on the shores of Loch Shieldaig, the original "Granny's Heeland Hame" perhaps?

An engaging sight is the village of Shieldaig seemingly clustered at the foot of the mighty Torridon mountains.

Ben Eighe and Liathach from Carn Breac.

Beached fishing vessel ending its days with grace, Lower Diabeg, Torridon.

The signature quartzite screes of Ben Eighe are luminescent in certain light. Here by Loch Coulin the scree is set off against native Rowan and Pine.

The A Gairbhe burn and Sgurr Dubh, Torridon.

Morning mist melts from the summit of the mighty Slioch, here presiding over a small spit of ancient Scots Pines.

Baosbheinn performs the evocation of a volcano, Torridon.

Inshore fisherman's art or
serendipitous abandon?
Loch Ewe.

Scarlet petals set off the lush green ferns, Inverewe Garden, NTS.

The trees of Inverewe's woodland
Garden have great stature.

Detail on the shore of the magnificent Gruinard Bay.

The grand sweep of Little Gruinard Bay halts many drivers.

An Teallach, The Forge in Gaelic, is a mountain held in great reverence by wilderness buffs. A classic Scottish mountain burn here offers some respite before the main assault on its complex series of summits.

Above: A couple of ponies grazing contentedly here at Scoraig on the shores of Little Loch Broom. The sugar loaf form of Sail Mhor creates the backdrop.

Opposite: A classic West Coast Sunset glows from the midge ridden but beautiful Loch Broom, Ullapool is just visible on the horizon.

Ullapool.

Ardmair and Loch Kanard, just north of Ullapool.

Heading into Coigach at sunset and the form of Stac Pollaidh is simply breathtaking.

The west shore of Loch Lurgain and the tantalising form of Stac Pollaidh is mimicked here by a small but graceful outcrop of bedrock set among the lush moorland flora of a Scottish summer.

Above: Cul Mor and Loch Sionascaig from Stac Pollaidh

Opposite: Achnahaird Beach near Achiltibuie here fully energised by a brisk northerly surf sets off the ethereal twin peaks of Cul Mor and Stac Pollaidh.

Semi derelict cottage and lone sheep, Achiltibuie.

The foreboding hulk of mighty Suilven rises behind Loch Culag, Lochinver.

Clinker-built dinghy and a scant copse of Scots Pine define the nature of Loch Assynt.

Assynt, a remote peninsula with an unusual status achieved when the resident crofters accomplished a buy out of the land. A beautiful coastal area, here epitomised by the abundant thrift and a view to the Old Man of Stoer.

Above: Polin Beach is a delectable place, a near neighbour of the more renowned Oldshoremore

Opposite: Ben Stack is an engaging and singularly pointy little mountain which characterises this stunning part of Sutherland.

Sandwood Bay Sutherland is a great prize in the West Coast explorer's book, wild and restless, it is both captivating and serene.

Am Buachaille, in Gaelic "The Herdsman" this superb basalt stack adds generously to the exhilaration of any visit to Sandwood Bay.

Photo by Lorna Willock

Allan Wright – short biography

Born Dunoon, Argyll 1951, lived in Broomhill Glasgow until 1956, then he moved to the Midlands & Yorkshire before returning to Jordanhill, Glasgow from 1964 til 1970. He Studied Geology and Geography at St Andrews University until 1974. For the next ten years Allan worked in the Oil industry as a "Mud Engineer" first in the US, then the North Sea followed by Libya, Vietnam, Bangladesh then Norway before escaping to rural Galloway in the eighties to transform his photographic hobby into a career as a landscape photographer. He still lives near Castle Douglas with his family.

Allan has sought to illuminate the very special sense of place the landscape of Scotland offers and has generated a uniquely subtle style of perceiving objects and transient light both in the natural world and the world of architecture. Since 1985 Allan has run his own publishing business under the imprint Lyrical Scotland producing many hundreds of postcard designs, an annual output of 16 Scottish view calendars and has in print a total of 10 book titles of his work.

Books by Allan include:

On The Rigs – 1995	Allan Wright & George Gunn
Galloway – 1999	Allan Wright & Tony Bonning
Arran – 2001	Allan Wright & Tony Bonning
Argyll – 2003	Allan Wright & Michael Russell (Birlinn)
The Trossachs – 2003	Allan Wright & Rennie McOwen (Birlinn)
Edinburgh – 2006	Allan Wright & Elizabeth Fraser
Mull & Iona – 2006	Allan Wright & Bill Clegg
Perthshire – 2007	Allan Wright & Felicity Martin
Glasgow – 2008	Allan Wright & Jack McLean
Scotland's West Coast – 2008	Allan Wright